EARTH'S CHANGING LANDSCAPE

Rivers in Action

Mary Green

W

FRANKLIN WATTS
LONDON•SYDNEY

This edition 2006

Franklin Watts
338 Euston Road
London NW1 3BH

Franklin Watts Australia
Hachette Children's Books
Level 17/207 Kent Street
Sydney NSW 2000

Series editor: Sarah Peutrill
Series designer: Simon Borrough
Art director: Jonathan Hair
Picture researcher: Juliet Duff
Illustrations: Ian Thompson
Series consultant: Steve Watts, FRGS, Principal Lecturer in
Geography Education at the University of Sunderland

A CIP catalogue record for this book is available from the British
Library

ISBN-10: 0 7496 6952 7
ISBN-13: 978 0 7496 6952 2
Dewey Classification: 551.48'3

Printed in Malaysia

Picture Credits:
Alamy Images: 33 Robert Harding Picture Library; 40 Leslie Garland
Picture Library. Corbis: 24 Robert Holmes; 32 Craig Aurness.
James Davis Travel Photography: 22, 25. Digital Vision: endpapers and
10, 18, 31, 34, 38, 39 (both). Ecoscene: 11 Joel Creed;14 David
Wootton Photography; 20 Colin Convoy; 27 (bottom) Christine
Osborne; 28–29 Alexandra Jones; 30 Chinch Gryniewicz; 42 Anthony
Cooper. Eye Ubiquitous: 8 Judyth Platt; 16, 37 (bottom) Julia Waterlow;
17, 23 J. B. Pickering; 19 Stephen Rafferty, 21 L. Fordyce (top), 26 Chris
Fairclough. Chris Fairclough Photography: 13.
Holt Studios International: 43 Mike Lane. Photodisc: 6, 21 (bottom).
Still Pictures: 12 Martin Hawes; 15, 36, 41 Mark Edwards; 18-19 Dylan
Garcia, 27 (top) Hjalte Tin; 29 Toby Adamson; 35 Paul Glendell, 37
(top) Jorgen Schytte. Front Cover: Ecoscene/Joel Creed.

Every attempt has been made to clear copyright. Should there be any
inadvertent omission, please apply to the publisher for rectification.

CONTENTS

RIVERS AND THE WATER CYCLE

Two-thirds of the Earth is covered with water. It is essential to all living things on the planet, but water also has a dramatic effect on the Earth's landscape. Rivers in particular have shaped many of the most spectacular landscape features of the world, provide fertile land for farming, and even determine where people live.

In the beginning
Water was formed from gases millions of years ago. Most of the water on Earth is salty and found in seas and oceans. The remainder is freshwater. Some of this is frozen into the great ice sheets of the Arctic and Antarctica, and mountain glaciers. The rest is found in lakes, rivers, streams and wetlands, in the soil as groundwater and in the atmosphere as water vapour.

Shifting water
We can think of all these places as storage houses for water, but water is constantly changing. It never remains the same because there are natural shifts between the water in the atmosphere and on the planet. This system, called the water cycle, keeps a balance between water in the air and on land.

Major rivers can even be seen from space. The Nile, the longest river in the world, is the thin strip to the left of this satellite image. It flows into the Mediterranean Sea, above.

Rivers Rivers have an important role in the water cycle because so much water, as rain or in other forms, finds its way into them.

A river is a natural flow of water moving in a channel towards the sea. As it does so it constantly changes and shapes the landscape. This process happens over thousands of years.

Some rivers flow into lakes and others into marshes or wetlands, but eventually all water ends up in the oceans.

Take it further

Investigate where rain collects after a shower. You can make a puddle map of your school yard for example.

◆ Show if the puddles are large or small quantities of water.
◆ Try to find out why they collect where they do.

How the water cycle works

1 Most rain falls on the seas, oceans, rivers and lakes. About a fifth falls on land. A certain amount of this will become groundwater by soaking into the soil and cracks in rocks. Some of the groundwater will find its way back into rivers. Water flows from rivers into the seas.

2 Plants use up some ground water and release some back into the air through a process called transpiration.

4 The clouds become thick with the droplets of moisture, until eventually these droplets are so heavy that the water falls as rain, or if it is cold enough, snow, sleet or hail. In this way the water cycle begins again.

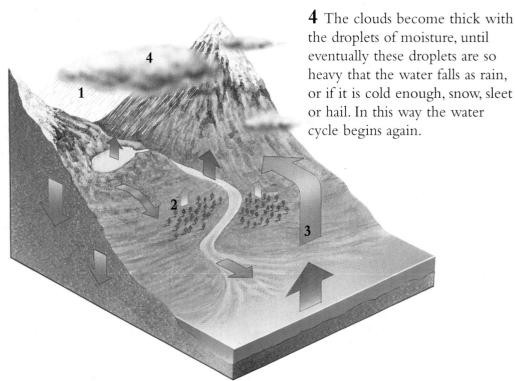

3 The sun warms surface water, both on land and on oceans, rivers and lakes. As it is warmed, it evaporates and rises as water vapour, then cools and condenses forming clouds.

THE RIVER'S COURSE

ost rivers begin their journeys high in the mountains. Some start as trickles of water from melting glaciers, others from lakes or springs. A river may flow for thousands of kilometres across a continent. It may join a larger river or other rivers may feed into it. It will pass through different landscapes and perhaps through towns and cities. But a river will always move from high to low ground because its water is governed by gravity and it will try to find the easiest route to the sea.

Mountain streams

When rain falls on a mountainside it seeps into the soil and crevices in rocks. Once these are full, the water spills onto the surface, creating streams that travel down the mountainside. These are the sources of rivers.

A mountain stream flows into a river below.

Follow it through: a river's course

Source is on high ground. Stream water is pulled down by gravity

Streams join to become a river, which also flows down mountains and hills

The upper course

A river's route has three stages. In its upper course it moves downstream, cutting a deep, narrow channel. The slope is often steep and rocky and there are many obstacles in the river's path.

The middle course

Here the river has a deeper and wider channel. Other smaller rivers join the main one, increasing the amount of water the river carries. It will flow fastest when the river is full and has strong currents. Zigzag shapes, called meanders, develop across the flood plain – the area that can flood after heavy rain.

Take it further
Where is your nearest river?

◆ Find it on a map and trace its course.
◆ What part of the river is in your locality? The upper, middle or lower course?
◆ What is the land surrounding the river used for?

The lower course

Towards the end of its course the river has less energy and becomes slower. The part of the river that enters the sea – or sometimes a lake – is called the mouth.

A river's course

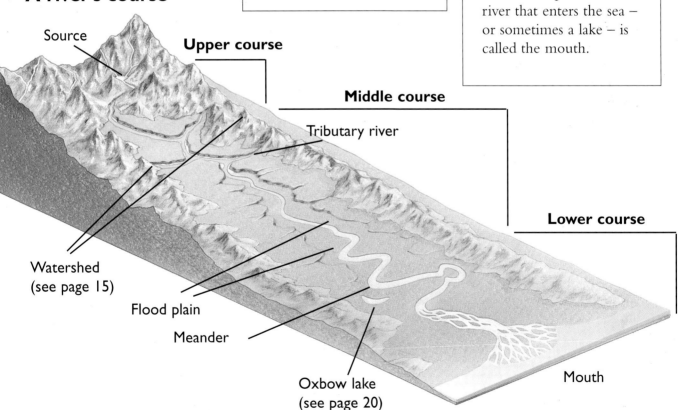

Source

Upper course

Middle course

Tributary river

Watershed (see page 15)

Flood plain

Meander

Oxbow lake (see page 20)

Lower course

Mouth

The river cuts a narrow channel downwards and moves on to less steep ground

Forms meanders across the gentler sloping land

Enters the sea or lake at its mouth

ERODING AND TRANSPORTING

A river may appear to be just a body of moving water, but there is a great deal of activity going on that affects its channel and surroundings.

Erosion As a river flows over rock and earth it wears it away, in a process called erosion. This takes place in several ways.

Corrasion occurs when material collides with the river's sides and bed. This also happens when pebbles grind into the bed causing potholes. They are carved into a circular shape by the river's action.

Corrosion occurs when rocks are dissolved by river water. This happens in particular to soft rocks such as chalk or limestone.

Another form of erosion is attrition. This happens when rocks, stones and gravel crash into each other and break up into smaller pieces. Material worn away from the upper course of the river travels downstream, causing more erosion further down.

Finally, there is hydraulic action. This happens when the force of water is so great it sweeps away materials from the sides and the bed of the river.

Fast flowing water can erode the bed and sides of the river.

Follow it through: erosion

River flows quickly and picks up material ▶ Material hits the river's banks ▶ The banks and bed are eroded

Take it further

Collect some river water and sediment in a jar. Shake or stir it and watch it settle.

◆ What materials can you see?
◆ Which settle first?
◆ Which do you think could be transported by suspension? (Always take care if you are visiting a river site.)

Transportation

A river also moves its 'load' of rocks, pebbles, earth, gravel and other materials, from one place to another: a process called transportation. This takes four different forms as well.

Some materials are dissolved in the water and carried in solution. Other small, visible particles are often light enough to be carried in suspension in a fast-flowing river.

Saltation occurs when small stones, too heavy to be lifted by the flow, jump along the riverbed. At the same time larger rocks and stones are rolled or pushed along, becoming rounder and smoother, in a process called traction.

Fast and steep

The extent of erosion and transportation depends on several things: how much energy the river has, how much water it is carrying and how steep the land is. Erosion and transportation also work together: the material the river transports helps the river to erode.

The river's load gives the water its brown colour.

Eroded material breaks away from the banks and bed

This material is transported in the flow

Further erosion is caused by the river's load, as it flows along its course

DEPOSITING MATERIALS

As well as eroding and transporting material, the river also deposits. This happens whenever the water lacks the energy to carry its load. There are certain points on the river's course where this occurs.

A river makes a looping meander.

Meanders These are bends or loops in the river created across the flood plain as the current swings from side to side. The water flows at different rates – quickly on the outside of a bend and more slowly on the inside. This causes the river to erode its banks on the outside, while dropping material on the inside, so increasing the size of the bends. Over time the meanders become larger and shift their position, changing the natural landscape.

Follow it through: deposition

River has less energy on some parts of its course

It drops its load

Spilling onto the flood plain

A river carries its greatest load when it is full, after heavy rain.

If a river floods, its energy falls, and it can no longer carry its load. Some is deposited on the river's banks, forming natural embankments called levees. Elsewhere, silt – fine soil – is dropped across the flood plain, helping to create fertile soil for farming.

Estuaries

Material is also deposited at a river's mouth, where it enters the sea. Here, some rivers create estuaries – where deposits of silt and sand create mudflats or sandflats. If the river splits around the mudflats into channels, a delta is created (see page 21). Estuaries are flooded by the sea, but at low tide the mudflats are visible.

Deposits of silt have created mudflats at this river's estuary.

Lakes

A river that has its mouth at a lake also drops its load. Its energy decreases as the water deepens. The heavier materials are dropped first, followed by the finer silt.

These silt deposits can build up into layers, or jetties, over many years. On the Gippsland lake system in New South Wales, Australia, silt jetties formed around one million years ago. They stretch in long lines far into Lake King. Because of their shapes they are called finger deltas or bird's foot deltas.

The material forms slopes at the inner bend of a meander

Over time silt builds up on the inner bend

The river continues to erode the bank of the outer bend.

The meander gets bigger

TRIBUTARIES AND DRAINAGE

A river is rarely just a single channel along its course. On its journey it is joined by other rivers, and may also split into separate channels itself. From source to mouth, rivers are ever-changing and dynamic.

Several tributaries flowing into this river create a shape like a tree with branches across the landscape.

Coming together, splitting apart

Smaller rivers that join the main river are called tributaries. High in the mountains these tributaries may be small streams called headwaters. Much larger tributaries, rivers in their own right, are found further along the river's course, on the flood plain. The point where rivers meet is known as a confluence. Finally, at the mouth, the river discharges into the sea, and may separate into channels called distributaries.

The Nile's tributaries

On the upstream section of the Nile there are two major tributaries, which join to form the main river.

The White Nile begins at Lake Victoria, in Uganda, and runs northward through lakes and swamps on a course of about 2,560 kilometres.

The Blue Nile flows 1,600 kilometres from Lake Tana in Ethiopia, and meets the White Nile at Khartoum in the Sudan. The main part of the River Nile then runs for another 3,000 kilometres to the Mediterranean Sea.

The drainage basin and watershed

The area of land drained by a river and its tributaries is called the drainage basin. This is the land that slopes down towards the river, with steep sides in the mountains and gentler inclines as the river passes through its course. The Nile has a drainage area of 2,881,000 square kilometres.

The ridge of land in between two drainage basins is called the watershed. The area shown on the diagram on page 9 represents a drainage basin with an upland watershed.

The Orinoco River is a tributary of the Amazon. Its basin extends over 150,000 square kilometres. It is divided between Brazil and Venezuela.

Take it further

On a map choose a major river, such as the Amazon or the Yangtze.

◆ Find its tributaries. What are their names?
◆ Find a confluence.
◆ How many major cities does it flow through?

The Giant Amazon

Some drainage basins are gigantic. The River Amazon is 6,450 kilometres long and although this is shorter than the Nile it drains more than 7,000,000 square kilometres of land. This is over two fifths of the South American continent and nearly two and a half times more area than the Nile.

The Amazon rises in the Andes Mountains and tumbles down in great waterfalls and rapids, dropping thousands of metres. Many tributaries join it over its course from west to east arriving at the Atlantic Ocean. At its mouth the Amazon is over 240 kilometres wide.

RIVER VALLEYS

Some of the most dramatic landforms are river valleys. These are shaped over thousands of years and have different characteristics according to where the valley occurs on the river's route. There are many kinds of river valleys, but they all follow the same basic pattern of development.

Tiger-leaping Gorge, a 'V'-shaped valley in China.

Highland valleys On its upper course, a river will cut deep into the land, eroding downwards so there is little or no valley floor. This, along with the weather's action, which erodes the valley's sides, helps to make a 'V' shape, giving rise to the name 'V'-shaped valley. Many of the steepest and longest river valleys are in the Himalayas of Asia. Some have sides that plunge over 1,500 metres.

Follow it through: valley erosion

River runs through a valley

Water erodes the valley sides

Drainage basin increases

Spurs

As the river erodes downwards, it begins to twist and turn around hard rock, forming sections of land, called spurs, jutting into the valley. The spurs alternate from side to side and, from a great height, they often look as if they should fit neatly into each other, like pieces in a jigsaw. This gives them the name of interlocking spurs.

Lesser gradients

Further changes occur as the river makes its way downhill. When tributaries flow into the river and its channel becomes wider, it erodes sideways into the river banks as well as eroding downwards. This creates a valley floor and flat land. Now there are slopes rather than steep gradients and a wider 'V'-shaped valley.

Moffat Valley in Scotland. The river meanders along the valley floor.

Lowland valleys

As the river flows nearer to the sea, its meandering course pushes out the valley sides still further. Some rivers, such as the Mississippi in the USA and the Hwang Ho in China, have huge meanders that sweep across the valley. These are created by the rivers' action, which is both eroding and depositing material (see pages 12–13). These processes increasingly widen the valley floor.

Over time the river creates its flood plain. On the river's lower course the valley sides can hardly be seen, if at all.

More water runs off into the river

River has more power

Valley is eroded further, including the river's floor

WATERFALLS AND RAPIDS

One of the most spectacular of all river features, and perhaps in all nature, has to be a waterfall. Some are special because of their beauty, particularly when they drop from a great height. Others stand out because of the great rush and power of the flowing water. A few of the greatest waterfalls are impressive for both reasons.

The creation of a waterfall
Waterfalls are created by erosion. The river meets hard rock, then flows onto soft rock. The water erodes soft rock far more quickly, so the hard rock is left extending out as a ledge that the water spills over.

A small upstream waterfall in the Swiss Alps.

Foz do Iguaçu Park Falls, Brazil.

Moving waterfalls
Waterfalls spill into a plunge pool, which is eroded by the water and the material it transports as it pours down. In addition, boulders and stones from the edge fall into the pool and the ledge breaks away. Consequently, over thousands of years, the waterfall slowly shifts backwards.

Waterfalls can be tiny or immense. The Iguaçu River in Brazil forms a vast network of 275 separate waterfalls in the Foz do Iguaçu National Park. Plunging some 82 metres, they are some of the world's most impressive and beautiful waterfalls.

Follow it through: waterfalls

> River meets hard rock and soft rock

> Soft rock is eroded first

Case study: Niagara Falls, USA and Canada

River landscape features can be so dramatic and important that they become borders between one country and another. The Niagara Falls form a boundary between Canada and the USA. It consists of two main waterfalls, separated by Goat Island.

Influence on the area

Although only the 49th highest waterfall in the world, the Niagara Falls is the third greatest in terms of the power and volume of water. Its spectacular beauty makes it one of North America's major tourist attractions. This has caused the whole area to be developed for tourism, including parks, golf-courses, museums, shops and restaurants. Without the draw of the waterfall, the area would be very different.

Great Gorge Adventure Rapids, Niagara, Canada.

Rapids Rapids are created in a similar way to waterfalls. Where water rushes over bands of soft and hard rock on the river bed, the soft rock is worn away first. This leaves the hard rock to form a series of steps, like small waterfalls, on the river bed. Where there are steep steps, the eddies and currents can be fierce. Eventually the steps may become so steep that the rapids develop into a waterfall. Usually a region of rapids remains in the stretch immediately upstream from a waterfall, as at Niagara Falls.

Rapids like these are used for recreational or sporting activities such as white water rafting. The River Ocoee in Tennessee, USA, was once harnessed for water power. An artificial channel called a flume diverted the water to a power station, but this made the river unusable for people. The flume was eventually disbanded and the rapids restored.

| A ledge of hard rock is left jutting out | A waterfall is created | The ledge breaks away | Waterfall moves backwards |

OXBOWS AND DELTAS

Other spectacular landscape features are formed by the river's action further along its course.

Crescent-shaped lakes As the river zigzags across its flood plain, eroding land on the outer bend of the meander and depositing material on the inner (see pages 12-13), the loops it makes become circular and very large, with a narrow neck.

At a certain point the river cuts through the land at the neck of the loop, taking a straight, more direct course. A crescent-shaped lake called an oxbow is left behind (see diagram on page 9).

An aerial view of a tightly meandering river in Borneo. The river will eventually cut through at the 'neck', leaving behind the meander as an oxbow lake.

Follow it through: oxbow lakes

River erodes on its outer bend

It deposits on its inner bend

Meanders form

Mud and sand

Further deposits of mud and sand, called deltas, can form around estuaries. Triangular-shaped deltas occur over vast areas at the mouths of large rivers, where the currents are slow and there are no strong tides to wash the silt away. Because the deposits block up the mouth, the river splits into two channels that flow around the blockage.

Further channels occur in this way as the water attempts to reach the sea.

The Mississippi delta between Houma and Grand Isle, Louisiana.

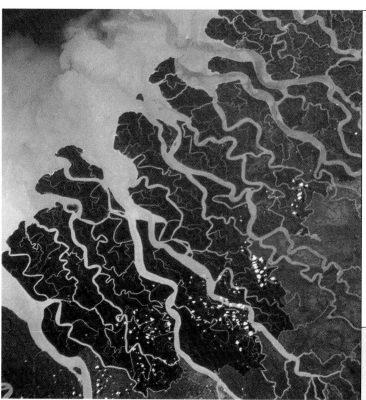

Stagnant rivers

The River Ganges, in India, is estimated to carry 900,000 tonnes of sediment daily. Not surprisingly, its huge low-lying delta is continually growing and the landscape changes as channels silt up. Parts of the delta are made up of older deposits that have been cut into by the current distributary rivers.

At some point, probably a few centuries ago, the main outlet of the river moved from west to east, leaving the western part as a 'dying' delta of stagnant rivers and poor soils that are not renewed by fertile silt.

A satellite view of the mouth of the River Ganges in Bangladesh. Silt deposits have been cut into separate banks by the many distributary rivers.

In time meanders become bigger

The sides of the loop get closer

The neck of the loop is cut through

An oxbow lake is left behind

WHERE SHALL WE SETTLE?

Today we think of towns and cities as part of the urban landscape. But many began as small communities that date back hundreds or even thousands of years. Why people chose a particular site above others is complicated. But different river sites, as well as providing a water supply and a potential transport route, offer certain benefits.

Two villages are connected by a bridge in South Sumatra, Indonesia.

A bridging point It was much easier to build a bridge across a river at some points than others. Lower down the river's course was generally better. Settlements at these points could become important centres linking different places.

South Sumatra has a gigantic set of rivers, some big and some small, that link the scattered settlements of the country. Many of these settlements lie by bridging points and connect the country's roads.

Case study: Rotterdam

Settlements sited at the mouth of a river often grew into harbours or ports.

Small beginnings

Rotterdam began as a fishing village around a dam on the tiny River Rotte, giving rise to the name 'Rotterdam'. At first it grew slowly but its harbour, which was easy to navigate, and its position on the North Sea helped trade to develop.

Expansion

The city expanded around the three rivers, the Sclhelde, Rijn and Maas, that connect to the River Rhine. Rotterdam is now the largest port in the world. Cargo is transported to and from the port, along a network of roads, railways and waterways, which link it to most of the major European cities. Thus its position by a river has dramatically affected the development of the area.

An estuary A settlement at the mouth of a river could also have advantages. The sea was near for fishing and boats could sail inland. One disadvantage, however, was that the community could be easily attacked by enemy vessels.

Lisbon, the capital city of Portugal, is situated on the north bank of the estuary of the Tagus River. The city has probably been occupied since around 750BCE and, owing to its ideal location, became one of the great seaports of Europe in the 15th and 16th centuries. Although the estuary provided Lisbon with many benefits, the city's proximity to the coast has meant that it has had a long history of invasion.

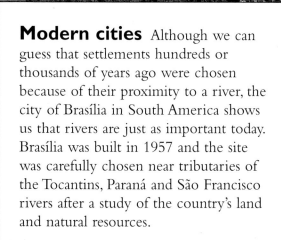

A defensive site Rivers could provide protection as well. A site in the bend of a meander meant that the settlement was surrounded on three sides by water, making it harder to attack.

Mosel, in Germany, is built around a defensive site of a river meander.

Modern cities Although we can guess that settlements hundreds or thousands of years ago were chosen because of their proximity to a river, the city of Brasília in South America shows us that rivers are just as important today. Brasília was built in 1957 and the site was carefully chosen near tributaries of the Tocantins, Paraná and São Francisco rivers after a study of the country's land and natural resources.

RIVER SETTLEMENTS

Many major settlements had their beginnings by rivers, but although a site was perhaps chosen for its easy access to food or for its defensive position, rivers may continue to be just as important to towns and cities today.

Egypt's growth

The Nile, the world's longest river, has seen settlements grow around it for thousands of years. Floods created fertile land for farming and a regular supply of food meant that communities grew.

The northern part of the Nile flows through Egypt, one of the longest continuously settled places on Earth. There, in the river valley, the ancient Egyptian civilization began around 7,000 years ago. Today Egypt is still centred on the Nile. Some 99 per cent of Egypt's population lives in the Nile's basin and depend on agriculture, which requires irrigation from the river.

Case study: New Orleans, USA

The city of New Orleans once owed much of its success to the Mississippi River, the longest river in the USA. After its discovery in 1541, the Mississippi became a major transport route for goods such as crops and furs, and the busy port of New Orleans grew up around it. Later the river provided recreational facilities such as boating, fishing and swimming. This attracted tourists to the city for many years so the Mississippi continued to be New Orleans' lifeline.

Hurricane Katrina

On 29 August 2005, Hurricane Katrina hit New Orleans. The storm broke flood defences and caused floodwater to pour into the low-lying city. By 31 August, about 80% of New Orleans was underwater and the city was evacuated. Many people have now returned but it may be many years before the city fully recovers.

New Orleans before the hurricane.

Follow it through: new settlers

Land taken by settlers

Not always enough water for the growing population

Large irrigation projects introduced

Running dry Rivers are often the main reason why an area is settled in hot, dry regions, but sometimes, during droughts, rivers dry up. In order to survive, people have learned how to adapt the environment.

The River Murray, which runs through parts of the south-west Australian outback has a history of drying up. The area was first settled by Aborigines, who were thought to have lived along parts of the river for at least 25,000 years. During periods when the river dried up, the Aborigines conserved water in rock holes.

River irrigation has enabled vineyards to prosper in Australia.

Surviving the climate With the coming of European settlers, the Aborigines lost their lands. The River Murray now became the main transport route bringing goods to the new settlements. But the settlers faced the same problems as the Aborigines – surviving in the harsh climate.

Only when large-scale irrigation projects were introduced did any of these settlements survive. By taking the water from the river and pumping or channelling it onto the land, fertile soil was created. The region now provides most of South Western Australia with huge quantities of produce from orchards and vineyards. The river has allowed settlements to grow and prosper despite the harsh climate.

Land becomes fertile

Orchards and vineyards flourish

Area changes and becomes an agricultural region

IRRIGATING FARMLAND

Rivers are essential to farmers. Over thousands of years farmers have developed many ways to use rivers for irrigation, but it is probably the most modern methods that have had the greatest impact on rivers and the landscape.

Different irrigation methods

In the simplest forms of irrigation, water is drawn from a river and distributed over the land by means of small ditches. This method is used by individual farmers in arid countries all over the world.

Larger communities have more complicated systems in which rivers supply canals, and the canals form branches that carry the water to all parts of the cultivated region. The largest irrigation systems involve the development of entire river basins with canals, dams and other major engineering works. They have a massive impact on the landscape.

An aerial view of a river meandering through irrigated land in Ethiopa. A single river can be used to irrigate a vast area of land.

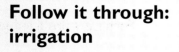

Follow it through: irrigation

Where there is little rainfall, farmers take river water

This is passed through channels to irrigate the soil

Supplying a large area

Modern irrigation systems, supplied by rivers, are capable of feeding millions of hectares of land. Most of the irrigation water in India and Pakistan is supplied by tributaries of the Indus and Ganges rivers and is distributed by one of the best developed canal systems in the world. This system irrigates a vast area of land.

Irrigation problems
Modern irrigation systems control the flow of a river, so there is always just enough water. This prevents flooding, which although an advantage, can also cause problems.

The Nile is Egypt's main source of irrigation. In the past the annual floods irrigated the area and carried silt – fine fertile soil – onto the land. Modern systems now provide year-round irrigation, but stop the annual flooding. This reduces the silt renewal and so farmers have to buy expensive fertiliser to enrich the soil instead.

Irrigation channels can have mixed results. This Egyptian field (above) has become waterlogged due to over-irrigation and, without the annual flooding, there are fewer areas of fertile land like this flood plain in Luxor (below).

Crops can be watered all year round

No silt from regular flooding

Soil is less rich and there are fewer fish

Fertilisers are needed

DAMS

The first simple dams were clay or stone banks across rivers. Their purpose was to hold back the flow of water so that a small lake formed. This could be used to irrigate fields or trap fish. Such dams only had a limited effect on the surrounding landscape. Modern dams have many more functions and work on a much greater scale. As a result, they have more wide-ranging effects.

Modern dams These are huge, expensive projects that take many years to build. They are usually built in an upland area where there is a steep-sided valley, gorge or canyon, some hard rock and a regular flow of water. The dam holds back the river so that the water level behind it rises. The surrounding landscape is flooded and a deep reservoir or lake is created. The flow of water is usually controlled by sluice gates and the water can be used to irrigate land, prevent floods and generate power (see water power, page 30).

The problem with dams Dams have many benefits, but they also create problems. The main one is that they change the landscape beyond recognition. Towns and villages can be wiped out by the creation of a lake, and wildlife habitats destroyed.

Because the dam blocks the river, it prevents the navigation of shipping and migration by fish, although special channels can be built to help. The creation of an artificial lake can bring benefits, however, such as a providing a site for recreation and encouraging wildlife.

A dam scheme in Australia has caused this river to flood rainforest and bush land.

Follow it through: dams

Dams block rivers

They hold back the flow of water

A lake is created behind the dam

28

Take it further

Find out the effect the Three Gorges Dam has on the town of Yichang.

◆ What happens to the people and local businesses?
◆ What could the Chinese government do about this?

Case study: the Three Gorges Dam, China

The Three Gorges Dam is a massive, controversial project, begun in 1992, and due to be completed in 2009. It is being built at Sandouping on the River Yangtze, one of the longest rivers in the world. The project is intended to create electricity and prevent flooding. It will also allow ships to pass through the three gorges – Wu, Xiling and Qutang – more easily.

Landscape changes

But of course there will be a huge impact on the surrounding area, particularly when the land is flooded to create the lake. Villages and towns will be drowned in the rising waters, and 2,000,000 people will need new homes. Factories and industries will disappear. Wildlife will be destroyed. The area is also an earthquake zone and there are fears that a serious earthquake might undermine the dam. Millions of litres of water could be released with disastrous results.

The Three Gorges Dam is a massive engineering project

The flow of water from the lake into the river is controlled

Water is used for power and irrigation

Landscape is changed

A traditional waterwheel for irrigating fields in Germany.

WATER POWER

River water has been used to generate power for thousands of years. The waterwheel was first used by the Romans and became a familiar feature of many landscapes until the 20th century. Today, dams are used to create hydroelectric power, dramatically affecting the rivers and the surrounding landscape.

Waterwheels Waterwheels were mainly used in the past to run mills to grind grain into flour. For small scale use they were clean and reliable. The small millpond (created as the river was dammed) not only provided the water to drive the wheel, but also attracted birds, frogs, dragonflies and other creatures.

Compared to modern systems of water power, the waterwheel had little impact on the river and the surrounding environment.

Hydroelectric power Modern methods use water to create hydroelectric power – energy produced by falling water. In mountain regions where the water is fast flowing, its energy can be directly used to drive turbines and create electricity.

Usually once a dam has been built, the water in the reservoir behind the dam is controlled by sluice gates. When these are opened water rushes out, passes down pipes and drives a turbine that produces electricity in a generator. The electricity is sent along pylons to homes, factories and offices.

Case study: Waikato River, New Zealand

The Waikato is New Zealand's longest river, on which eight dams with power stations have been built, leading to great changes in the surrounding landscape.

Using the lakes

The stations provide much of the power for New Zealand's North Island. The artificial lakes, however, have been given an extra purpose by becoming popular recreational areas that attract thousands of visitors each year. Before the development of the dams, the fast-moving river only allowed for a limited range of activities.

Take it further

Carry out some research into two different dams – a small one and a large one.

◆ How much power do they each generate?
◆ What effect on the local environment does each one have?
◆ Which do you think is more successful?

Water passing through the Victoria Dam in Sri Lanka creates a massive force that is harnessed for hydroelectric power.

Alternative energy

Hydroelectric power has certain advantages over other ways of producing energy. It does not rely on fossil fuels, such as coal, which create pollution. It is also a renewable source. This means it can be replaced and is not constantly being used up.

However, its main disadvantage is its reliance on dams, which disrupt the local landscape and are costly to build.

RIVERS AS WATERWAYS

Rivers have been used for transport for thousands of years. They provided a natural network across land when roads were only tracks. However, travelling by river was limited because rapid and shallow waters were often impossible to navigate. Consequently people found ways to alter rivers to overcome these problems.

The Mississippi River, the longest river in the USA, has long been an important transportation route. In parts it is over two kilometres wide, and its depth ranges between 15–30 metres.

Straighter and deeper Rivers such as the Mississippi have been straightened to cut out meanders. Channels have been deepened by removing the silt deposits – a process called dredging. These measures increase the river's flow, which allows vessels to travel more quickly and directly.

But these kinds of changes come at a price. Deepening and shortening the river's channel can increase the volume and speed of the water downstream. This means that the chances of flooding in heavy rain become greater. In the case of the Mississippi, erosion increased as the flow became quicker, and the river dumped more silt downstream. So the river began to meander once again.

Canals These are constructed waterways that can bypass obstacles to connect one river with another or a river with a sea. They are massive engineered constructions and may even include aqueducts – bridges that carry water – to take vessels over valleys and ravines.

Take it further

Using a map of the country, plan a route for a new canal that connects two river systems.

◆ What problems will you have to overcome?
◆ What landscape features will be lost?
◆ What benefits might it bring?

A narrowboat passes over Pontcysyllte Aqueduct on the Shropshire Union Canal in Clwyd, Wales, UK. This canal, like many others, is now largely used by leisure boats.

Major canals

Canals have given us a network of water transport to carry cargo across continents. The Panama Canal connects the Atlantic and the Pacific oceans; the Europa Canal connects the rivers Rhine and Danube. The Rhine is also linked to the Saone, the main tributary of the Rhone, by canals. These waterways are very important for shipping. Barges carrying raw materials constantly use them.

Building canals

The building of canals causes widespread destruction of landscapes and habitats. Disused canals can also cause problems as they attract waste and pollution. Such canals can be renewed, however, and may become popular leisure areas.

WHEN RIVERS FLOOD

Flooding rivers are a major concern. They occur for many reasons, but can often be caused by a landscape change, such as deforestation, the building of hard surfaces, or the restructuring of a river's course.

The River Jhelum in Srinagar, Kashmir, has a history of flooding. Many people have now made their homes on houseboats.

When floods happen

River floods may occur in any season, but they are more likely in spring and in winter. In the spring, the main causes of flooding are heavy rains and a rise in temperature. In the winter, the main factors are frozen soil, deep snow and a thaw. Floods during winter and spring occur on major rivers and affect large areas.

Follow it through: deforestation

Trees are cut down

Soil is no longer held by tree roots

Rainy days Rivers often overflow in heavy rain. This can happen when the ground is already waterlogged. The excess water runs into rivers, which rise and burst their banks. The area of land that is most likely to flood is across the flood plain, since this is the lowest lying area on a river's course. This is also the area where many people live. Settlements originated on flood plains because the soil was fertile and the land flat.

The increased building of roads, walkways, car parks and other hard surfaces, means that excess water is not absorbed by the soil. Instead it runs into drains and into the rivers, eventually causing flooding. Heavy rain combined with a high tide can be especially destructive.

Deforestation
The destruction of forests can also have an effect on rivers. When trees are cleared, their roots no longer hold the soil and this can cause erosion. Heavy rain then washes away the topsoil into the rivers. The soil builds up, the rivers become blocked and flooding occurs. This is a particular problem in countries that are being cleared of rainforest.

Changing a river's course
Dramatic changes to a river by people can also have unforeseen effects. The Netherlands suffered from catastrophic floods in 1993 and 1995. These can be traced to the straightening of the upper Rhine to improve shipping conditions. This led to rising waters flowing downstream more rapidly (see page 40).

Floods can cause millions of pounds worth of damage to homes and other property.

Benefits and disasters
Floods can be beneficial, too. Bangladesh experiences both the benefits and the disasters of flooding from rivers and the sea. The country is situated on the flat, broad Ganges delta. Like the land along the Nile, fertile soil is produced by the silt carried in the floodwaters, so it is good for farming. Farmers are able to produce enough food for the region's large population.

However, the rainy season, known as the monsoon, can bring disaster. The rivers burst their banks and submerge farmland in a great sweep of water. Thousands can die along with their livestock, and crops can be destroyed.

In response, people have turned to ways to defend against flooding.

Heavy rain washes
topsoil into rivers

Soil builds up in
the river

Rivers become blocked and
flood during heavy rain

FLOOD CONTROL

Flooding can never be completely prevented but it can be controlled, especially with modern flood forecasting methods. These involve studying how a river is likely to react during particular kinds of weather. Satellites send pictures showing conditions in the atmosphere. Data is collected, fed into a computer and a forecast is made. Flood protection is then used at the right time.

The Thames Flood Barrier was opened in 1982 to prevent flooding in central London during high tides and winds.

Dams and barriers

Large scale 'hard engineering' projects such as dams and barriers, which hold back a river and manage its flow, can be highly effective at flood control. The Thames Flood Barrier in London is a striking landmark across the river. It has steel gates that can be opened or closed and can endure pressure of up to 9000 tonnes.

Concrete levees Other hard-engineering methods such as dykes or concrete embankments (levees) are built alongside rivers to keep the river in its course. About 78,000 square kilometres of the flood plain of the Mississippi River are protected by levees and other structures. They have to be constantly renewed or increased in height.

Follow it through: soft-engineering flood control

Marshlands renewed

They take in and hold rainwater

Women in Bangladesh building river embankments by hand.

Take it further

Many of those living on the world's great deltas, such as those in Bangladesh and China, depend on farming. Find out what methods are being proposed to help reduce flooding.

◆ Are they nature-friendly or not?
◆ What effect might they have on the landscape?

Dredging Because of the enormous load of silt that the Hwang Ho or Yellow River, in China, carries, it is very wide and shallow. This has led to so many disastrous floods that the river is often called 'China's Sorrow'.

To prevent further floods the river's bed has been dredged to lower it, and embankments have been built. In some stretches during high rainfall the water level between the embankments may be nine metres above the surrounding plain.

Such changes have a huge impact on the environment so alternative 'soft-engineering' methods, such as terracing and reforestation, are becoming more popular.

Dredging the Yellow River to remove silt.

Controlling run-off Terracing is a form of irrigation usually found in upland areas. It involves cutting a series of steps into the hillside, so that the farmed land is almost level, rather than on a slope. As well as being a good farming method, it can also be used as flood control: rainwater is collected so run-off into rivers is limited.

Other methods to control water run-off and prevent flooding include planting trees on hillsides and digging small irrigation channels on farmland.

Protecting wetlands In the past draining wetlands – low-lying marshy regions – led to flooding, since the marshland acts as a reservoir for heavy rains. Conservation projects to renew wetlands therefore help to prevent flooding, and also revive the natural vegetation and support wildlife.

Like dams and barriers these soft-engineering projects can alter landscapes. However, they do so in a way that encourages sensible farming and balances the needs of the people, plants and animals in the environment.

Less water run-off into rivers

Reduces flooding

Environment for wildlife restored

POLLUTED RIVERS

Rivers have always been used to dump waste, but as the world's population has grown, pollution has increased. Despite greater awareness, pollution still reaches rivers and groundwater in several ways, damaging the landscape and environment.

Chemicals discharged into a river affect the water and can harm plant and animal life.

Sources of pollution The main sources of river pollution are farm waste – especially fertilisers – industrial waste, oil and even warm water. Waste tips also produce poisons that can seep into groundwater. All these things change the water, usually decreasing the oxygen available to support plant and animal life.

Follow it through: cost of river pollution

Farmers and industries want to dispose of waste cheaply

Cleaning up rivers Several things can be done to improve river quality. Fines for industrial pollution can be strictly enforced. Natural farming methods that do not use artificial fertilisers, such as organic farming, can be encouraged. Greater recycling of rubbish is also important.

If a polluted river is cleaned nature quickly returns. British rivers were once some of the worst in Europe. Many are now cleaner than they have been for 150 years. This is partly due to the decline in heavy industry but also due to stricter pollution controls and programmes to clean up rivers.

Industrial waste pumped into rivers can harm wildlife.

Volunteers clear dumped waste from a river's edge.

Case study: the Illinois River, USA

The surrounding flood plains of the Illinois River are mainly used for raising crops. Formerly, the river was highly productive: it produced 10 per cent of the US freshwater fish catch. By the 1970s, the same stretch of river produced only 0.32 per cent of the total freshwater fish harvest.

This was due to two major factors: the diversion of Chicago's sewage from Lake Michigan to the river, and the high level of agriculture – the fertilisers used caused a reduction in the oxygen levels. This pollution is slowly being reversed with new sewage treatment methods.

Fertilisers and chemicals dumped into rivers

Supply of freshwater decreases and wildlife harmed

Costly river clean-up is needed

The junction of the River Rhine and the Mosel in Germany.

Rivers are not only damaged by pollution. Changing the course of the river, building dams, embankments and large irrigation projects often have unexpected outcomes for the river and the surrounding landscape. Many governments now accept that controlling rivers for human use should be balanced against the damage this can cause to the environment.

Rhine 2020 Attempts to improve the Rhine caused disastrous flooding (see page 35). Now a project called Rhine 2020 has been undertaken to protect and renew the river. Its name refers to the time span of the project – 20 years from its start in 2000.

The aims of the project are to lower the water levels on the straightened stretch of the Rhine, and restore wetlands, which are a natural water purifier and help reduce flooding (see pages 42–43). Already, improvements have been made to the water quality of the river. Wildlife along the riverbanks is starting to return.

However the Rhine is still a major waterway. Ensuring the river revives at the same time as maintaining it as a transport route requires careful planning.

Follow it through: changes to a river bank

Trees are felled on a river bank

Giant reeds grow

Reeds block up the river and cannot provide shade

Take it further

Find out how your nearest river is managed.

◆ Is it polluted or clean?
◆ Who is responsible for managing the river?
◆ What are their plans for the future?
◆ How will this affect the river and surrounding landscape?

Surrounding landscape

Another way to protect a river is to ensure that its surroundings are preserved or renewed.

The Santa Clara River in Southern California is protected by an environmental management plan. The plan involves limiting future building, particularly across the flood plain, and planting trees to replace the overhanging willows and cottonwood forests that have been felled in the past. The loss of these trees reduced the shade on the river, making the water temperature rise and the chemical balance of the river change. This allowed algae to flourish on the surface of the water. Algae starved fish and other wildlife in the river of oxygen and many died. The replanting plan has reversed this effect and the river is now healthy and teeming with life.

Changing population

Other rivers are renewed less by design than by a simple change of circumstance. The upper Po Valley in Italy lost two thirds of its population in the 1960s due to migration to cities. The River Po's waters have been renewed and wildlife has returned.

The clear, fresh waters of the River Po, Italy. The changing population has helped to renew all sections of the river.

Water temperature rises

Algae flourishes

Fish and other wildlife are starved of oxygen

River renewal is needed

PROTECTING WETLANDS

The regeneration of wetlands is one way to prevent flooding, but they are in themselves very important habitats. Wetlands are low-lying marshy regions, fed by fresh water from rivers or streams and from tides near the coast. They support a wide variety of plant and animal life.

Wetlands and fish

From prehistoric times people have used marshes for food for themselves and their animals.

It is estimated that 80 to 90 per cent of the fish eaten throughout the world today depend on shallow coastal waters. Shrimp, crabs, oysters, and clams all depend on tidal and freshwater marshes for food and shelter, and in turn the fish attract many bird species.

The Burdekin wetland complex in North Queensland, Australia.

Case study 1: The Great Fen, East Anglia, UK

A great stretch of land across the eastern side of England was once covered by marshland called the Fens. It was first drained by the Romans and much of it has been used for farming ever since.

Big project

The Great Fen Project aims to restore some of this marshland, making it the largest conservation project in the UK for over 100 years. It will connect two important habitats, Woodwalton Fen and Holme Fen, making one large site. Farmland has been bought and drains and ditches that kept the land dry for crops will be blocked to increase the water level. Extra water can be pumped from nearby rivers. It is hoped that natural fen grasses will reappear, followed by fen reeds and later plants such as fen violets. As the habitat is slowly recreated, the area should become a haven for many birds and animals.

Follow it through: renewing wetlands

Farmland is purchased ➤ Drains and ditches blocked

Case study 2: The Everglades, Florida, USA

The Everglades is an unusual area of wetland. It is a shallow but wide area that creeps slowly through Southern Florida to the Gulf of Mexico. It has been called the 'river of grass' and there is nowhere else on Earth quite like it. Great sweeps of grasses and mangrove forests hide endangered species such as alligators.

Wetland loss

For many years the Everglades was drained and developed and the Kissimmee River, which fed it, was straightened and canalled. Some 50 per cent of the Everglades was lost.

Restoration

Now it is a vast nature reserve, which is internationally valued. Projects to maintain and restore further areas of the Everglades are being proposed.

Working with rivers

There is now a greater awareness of the need to restore rivers and waterways. This in turn renews the landscape, sometimes returning it to the way it once was thousands of years ago. Sustaining rivers also means that they can still be used as valuable resources. But to do this it must be recognised that rivers are dynamic. They are constantly changing and not easily tamed. The key is to work with, not against, them.

The Everglades is a wilderness that is unique in the USA. Its diverse habitats support a huge array of wildlife. Some plants and animals do not exist anywhere else in the country.

The water level rises, creating marshland

Extra water can be pumped from rivers

Wildlife habitats return

GLOSSARY

Algae Simple green plants that grow on ponds and rivers.

Attrition Erosion caused by rocks crashing into each other.

Channel The passage between two banks along which a river flows.

Condensation Droplets of water from the air that form when the temperature falls.

Confluence The place where two rivers meet.

Conservation Protecting the environment.

Corrasion Erosion caused by rocks colliding with a river bed and banks.

Corrosion Erosion caused by chemicals in river water dissolving rock.

Cottonwood trees Tall trees with seeds covered in cotton-like hairs.

Defensive site A site that offers protection from attack.

Deposition Material that is dropped by a river.

Dykes Embankments built to keep a river in its channel to control flooding.

Drainage basin The area drained by a river and its tributaries.

Delta Low, flat land formed by silt deposits at a river's mouth.

Erosion The process of being slowly worn away.

Estuary The mouth of a river that widens as the river flows into the sea.

Evaporation When water changes from liquid to vapour.

Flood plain The flat plain on each side of a river that often floods.

Glacier A slow moving river of ice.

Gravity The force that pulls everything towards the Earth.

Groundwater Underground water stored in rock.

Habitat A natural environment for plants and animals.

Hard engineering Large-scale structural developments that change the environment.

Irrigation Watering farmland by means of channels and pumps.

Levees Embankments along a river.

Mangrove A tree that grows in swamps.

Meander A bend or loop in a river.

Mouth The place where a river flows into the ocean, sea, lake or swamp.

Oxbow lake A crescent-shaped lake formed when the loop of a river becomes cut off.

Precipitation Water that falls from clouds as rain, snow, sleet or hail.

Reservoir	A lake built to store water, sometimes behind a dam.
Recycle	To process and reuse waste.
Run-off	Rainwater carried away from an area by streams and rivers.
Suspension	When materials are carried by the flow of a river.
Saltation	When materials jump along a river bed.
Silt	Fine, fertile soil, which can be carried by a river.
Sluice gate	A gate for controlling the flow of water.
Soft engineering	Structural changes that work with the environment rather than against it.
Source	The place where a river begins.
Transpiration	Water vapour that passes into the air from plants and trees.
Transportation	The movement of materials by a river.
Tributary	A smaller river that flows into a larger river.
Watershed	The border between two drainage basins.

FURTHER INFORMATION

Environment Agency (UK)
The main public body for the environment in England and Wales, dealing with flooding and river and wetland conservation.

www.environment-agency.gov.uk

Rivernet (USA)
An organisation that supports local communities in their efforts to protect and restore rivers, lakes, wetlands and estuaries.

www.rivernetwork.org

International Rivers Network (USA)
A campaigning group that works to protect the world's rivers. Suitable for older pupils.

www.irn.org

National Geographic Society (USA)
A website that includes an interactive river system and river conservation activities.

www.nationalgeographic.com/geographyaction/rivers

World Wide Fund for Nature (WWF)
An organisation concerned with conservation. Suitable for older pupils.

www.panda.org

Other useful sites
These websites feature many topics, including user-friendly information about rivers.

www.socialstudiesforkids.com
www.bbc.co.uk/schools

Note to parents and teachers: Every effort has been made by the Publishers to ensure that these websites are suitable for children, that they are of the highest educational value, and that they contain no inappropriate or offensive material. However, because of the nature of the Internet, it is impossible to guarantee that the contents of these sites will not be altered. We strongly advise that Internet access is supervised by a responsible adult.

INDEX